GW00420313

NAME

ADDRESS

PHONE

FAX

E-MAIL

WEBSITE

NAME

ADDRESS

PHONE

FAX

E-MAIL

WEBSITE

NAME

ADDRESS

PHONE

FAX

E-MAIL

WEBSITE

USEFUL ADDRESSES

NAME

ADDRESS

PHONE

FAX

E-MAIL

WEBSITE

NAME

ADDRESS

PHONE

FAX

E-MAIL

WEBSITE

NAME

ADDRESS

PHONE

FAX

E-MAIL

WEBSITE

NAME

ADDRESS

PHONE

FAX

E-MAIL

WEBSITE

NAME

ADDRESS

PHONE

FAX

E-MAIL

WEBSITE

NAME

ADDRESS

PHONE

FAX

E-MAIL

WEBSITE

NAME ....

ADDRESS ....

....

PHONE ....

FAX ....

E-MAIL ....

WEBSITE ....

NAME ....

ADDRESS ....

....

PHONE ....

FAX ....

E-MAIL ....

WEBSITE ....

NAME ....

ADDRESS ....

....

PHONE ....

FAX ....

E-MAIL ....

WEBSITE ....

USEFUL ADDRESSES

NAME

ADDRESS

PHONE

FAX

E-MAIL

WEBSITE

NAME

ADDRESS

PHONE

FAX

E-MAIL

WEBSITE

NAME

ADDRESS

PHONE

FAX

E-MAIL

WEBSITE

NAME

ADDRESS

PHONE

FAX

E-MAIL

WEBSITE

NAME

ADDRESS

PHONE

FAX

E-MAIL

WEBSITE

NAME

ADDRESS

PHONE

FAX

E-MAIL

WEBSITE

NAME

ADDRESS

PHONE

FAX

E-MAIL

WEBSITE

NAME

ADDRESS

PHONE

FAX

E-MAIL

WEBSITE

NAME

ADDRESS

PHONE

FAX

E-MAIL

WEBSITE

NAME

ADDRESS

PHONE

FAX

E-MAIL

WEBSITE

NAME

ADDRESS

PHONE

FAX

E-MAIL

WEBSITE

NAME

ADDRESS

PHONE

FAX

E-MAIL

WEBSITE

NAME

ADDRESS

PHONE

FAX

E-MAIL

WEBSITE

NAME

ADDRESS

PHONE

FAX

E-MAIL

WEBSITE

NAME

ADDRESS

PHONE

FAX

E-MAIL

WEBSITE

NAME

ADDRESS

PHONE

FAX

E-MAIL

WEBSITE

NAME

ADDRESS

PHONE

FAX

E-MAIL

WEBSITE

NAME

ADDRESS

PHONE

FAX

E-MAIL

WEBSITE

NAME

ADDRESS

PHONE

FAX

E-MAIL

WEBSITE

NAME

ADDRESS

PHONE

FAX

E-MAIL

WEBSITE

NAME

ADDRESS

PHONE

FAX

E-MAIL

WEBSITE

NAME

ADDRESS

PHONE

FAX

E-MAIL

WEBSITE

NAME

ADDRESS

PHONE

FAX

E-MAIL

WEBSITE

NAME

ADDRESS

PHONE

FAX

E-MAIL

WEBSITE